POSITIVELY ROCKS

Paint it Forward!

KATIE CAMERON

THUNDER BAY
P·R·E·S·S

San Diego, California

Positive Rocks

Rocks painted with colorful art and positive messages are turning up everywhere. You may have heard of these "word rocks," read about them on social media, seen a feel-good news report, or even discovered a random "rock of kindness" for yourself. If you haven't heard of the kindness movement in one way or another—paying it forward, the power of positive thinking, the importance of gratitude—you must have been living under a rock!

Jokes aside, painting and sharing rocks is an activity that connects people worldwide, teaches kindness and positivity, and helps people become happier. Research shows that acts of kindness have real, lasting effects. A kind action, no matter how small, can inspire those on the receiving end to pass it on or "pay it forward." There's evidence that giving to and helping others increases the giver's happiness and well-being even more than that of the person receiving the kindness. Of course, human decency is a good enough reason to be kind, but science confirms that even little acts of kindness do have an impact on your health.

These are perfect reasons to "paint it forward!" Painting stones with encouraging words, inspiring messages, and colorful art can be a fun and meaningful way to help create a positive, happy life. Just one word can be very powerful: for those looking to live better lives or reach a goal, a single word can be used as a simple affirmation to focus on and guide a person's actions when making decisions.

Contents

Sharing Your Stones

What can you do with your stones after you paint them? Kindness doesn't have to cost anything, and often the simplest things have the biggest effect. You don't need to spend a lot of money or go to great lengths to create rocks that make a difference. Stones are a part of nature and are generally available wherever anyone lives, and the messages on the stones can be created with something as simple as a permanent marker.

Social media is a fantastic way to share your painted stones. It's an effective sharing tool that inspires people to create their own art on stones. Fellow rock-painters can come together in community forums or on individual or group pages to share photos of their artwork. An artist can even mail their stones to people who may be going through a tough time. This can be costly, but there are other interesting ways people can send their rocks out into the world.

There has been a huge rise in popularity of hide-and-seek-type games with painted rocks. Stones are painted with words of encouragement and positive messages, then left in public spaces to be found. The rock "dropper" does not usually know who will find the stone, but knowing someone will find the stone with their message and that it will hopefully make them smile is enough to create those happy feelings that come with performing small acts of kindness.

The underside of the stone will often have a web address or hashtag on it for further information. The person who discovers it can follow the web address or hashtag, which typically takes them to a website where the purpose and intent of the message is explained further. Besides the primary motive of brightening someone's day, the finder is often encouraged to take a photo of the stone themselves and post it online using the same hashtag, so everyone can share the artwork, see where it was discovered, and by whom.

If they like, the finder can keep the stone, though it is in the spirit of the movement to then hide a replacement painted rock of their own, which can bring joy to someone else's day. Alternatively, they can hide the stone in a new location. Anyone and everyone can join in by creating their own random rocks of kindness! A person doesn't need to find a painted rock or be a member of a group to paint their own rocks for hiding. Start your own webpage featuring your art, invent a unique tag that links to your page, and use it on your stones that you leave out to be found. Follow other inspiring accounts of rock painters on social media to bring you further joy and to spark more creative ideas.

Bear in mind that the stones should be appropriate for all ages, mustn't be offensive in any way, and shouldn't be left anywhere that could be hazardous or that could cause harm or injury.

Many areas have rock-painting groups: try searching online to find one. Suggest painting positive stones as a theme at a school or community art class. This activity is a wonderful way to help teach students about being kind to each other and the cycle of happy feelings and positive actions that result from simple altruistic deeds. There's no better way to learn than by doing, especially by doing something with such positive outcomes.

Getting Started

You will need a few extra things before you can get started on your activities.

YOU WILL NEED:
- Stones
- A suitable work space
- Paints
- Tools and brushes
- Clear finish

Stones

The best stones to paint on are smooth and free of cracks or holes. Stones that are too rough are not ideal because they can cause markers or pens to be worn down. If a stone has a bumpy surface, paint can also be problematic and clean line detailing is difficult to achieve. If you are going to gather your own stones, smooth stones are most commonly found along the shores of oceans and rivers. If this is not an option or you want to save time, smooth stones can also be purchased from craft stores.

Also keep in mind that the larger the stone, the longer it can take to complete.

IMPORTANT: Make sure it is okay to take the stones from your area. Some places have regulations to protect the environment against things such as erosion or risks to animal habitats, and in some places, it can also be culturally inappropriate. Ensure that you always ask permission if taking from private property.

Be sure to thoroughly clean all your rocks before you start. Rinse off the bulk of any mud or sand outside (not down the kitchen drain, or it can get blocked), and then give them a scrub in the sink with soap and water. Leave them to air-dry in a sunny location, such as a windowsill. Ensure the stones are free from any dust or debris and are completely dry before you begin.

When hiding your rocks, ensure that it is in a public space that allows for rock hiding. Popular places to hide rocks include parks, beside walking trails, and anywhere outdoors that is free for public use. Some places such as national parks prohibit taking or leaving stones, so it's best to check their guidelines first. Never hide your stones on private property without explicit permission.

Work Space

You will need a large, well-lit work space with enough room for you to paint, and that also has everything you need within arm's reach. Your station should be high enough to maintain good posture and be equipped with a comfortable chair.

To keep your work space neat and tidy, place a piece of cardboard or paper towel beneath your stone before you begin, and protect the remainder of your space with a drop cloth or old newspaper. The cardboard helps keep the underside of the stone clean and can also be useful if you wish to move the stone to another area to dry.

HANDY HINT

Painting stones can take some time, so be aware of the time you're spending and try not to sit for too long! Get up, stretch, and move around for ten minutes or so at least once an hour. Movement is good for your body's circulation and can also help you refocus on the rock at hand.

Paints

Regular craft or student-grade acrylic paint works very well for painting stones. It is nontoxic, fast-drying, and adheres well to a stone's surface. It is affordable and easy to clean up using a little soap and water.

You can easily create new color combinations with most acrylic paints. Mix paints in a small container to make new colors; add a little bit of black to colors to create darker shades, or add white to lighten them.

Drying time for acrylic paint can range from 5 to 15 minutes. The time is affected by several factors: how heavily it is applied, temperature, humidity, etc. It can take up to 24 hours for acrylic paint to "cure" to the point where it is completely dry and at maximum hardness. It is important not to touch the stone during this time or you risk smudging it or leaving fingerprints.

Pen Types

Gel Pens

Gel pens are available in a variety of colors and finishes. They create a bold, bright line in metallic, pastel, iridescent, neon, or sparkly ink. Gel pens can be used on all kinds of surfaces due to the thickness of the gel ink, which is made up of pigment suspended in a water-based gel. It is stickier than a typical ballpoint pen, and more opaque, meaning it can be used on both light and dark backgrounds.

However, gel ink is prone to smearing. Watch how you handle the stone and try not to brush your hand over any wet ink. Drying time for gel ink can vary depending on the type and brand, and how much gel ink you have used (heavier application will take longer). Give ink lots of time to dry on stone—20 minutes for light applications, and overnight for areas that have heavy coverage. To check if it is dry, carefully lay a soft tissue over it to see if any ink transfers. If the ink is taking a long time to dry, try a quick coating of spray finish to speed it up.

You can also use smudges to your advantage. For a light sheen of color or shimmer, scribble gel pen on the background, then use your finger or a brush to smear and spread the ink around to create a translucent, even coat. Use the same process for blending color transitions and for shading.

Though gel pens are largely opaque, you may find the color doesn't appear as bright or vivid on stone as it does on paper. This may be due to the porous nature of the stone as well as the moisture in the gel ink causing a darker color. Allow the ink and the surrounding area to dry fully: a hairdryer on low helps speed up the process! For a more vibrant appearance, apply a base coat of white paint first, then color over it in gel pen. The ink will be true to color and you will need fewer coats.

Store gel pens with the caps on tightly and wipe their tips with tissue after use. If your pen stops working, tap the tip lightly on scrap paper. If there is still ink, it should reflow after a few taps.

Permanent Markers

Permanent markers can be useful and save time when creating artwork on stone. They are available in various tip sizes, from extra-fine to extra-large, as well as in different tip shapes. Markers and pens have stable tips that give you more control than a paintbrush, and so they can be useful for any lettering on your rocks.

Bullet (round) tips are the most common for writing. A black round-tip marker is handy for going over the outlines of letters and other design elements.

Chisel-tip markers are wedge-shaped, with a broad and a narrow edge on the same tip. Depending on how you hold a chisel marker, you can create thick or thin lines (used in calligraphy or brush-style writing). Position the chisel tip at a 45-degree angle to the baseline. It is important not to alter this angle to create consistently angled letters.

Tools

There are a few tools that are useful when designing and painting rocks:

- **Pencil and eraser**—use these to sketch out ideas and designs on paper beforehand. Pencils can be used directly on the stone or on dry paint. Use an eraser to remove light markings when you're finished with them, or just paint over them.

- **Drawing compass and ruler**—you can use your eye to judge measurements, like center points or circles, but a ruler and compass make this faster and more accurate. These tools can help with guidelines used for hand-lettering spacing and proportions.

- **Dotting tools**—a dowel is perfect for dotting. You can use a dotting stylus or a nail-dotting tool: these handy devices can be found at craft stores, are inexpensive, and work well for dotting with acrylic paint. You can also use small round brushes to create dots, or you can make your own using an array of common household items. Needles, toothpicks, skewers, pencil ends: if it has a pointed tip, you can use it to paint dots. These rigid items allow greater precision and control than a brush.

- **Synthetic brushes**—pointed and "detail round" brushes are best for fine detailing, thin lines, dotting, and touch-ups. Use a larger round or flat brush when painting areas that need more coverage, like thick lines and base coats. Brushes with shorter handles and short, firm bristles are better for precise detailing. The amount of paint on the brush and how much pressure you use will also affect how paint is distributed on the stone.

Maintain brushes in good condition, keeping the bristles straight and together. Never let them dry with paint still on their bristles. Only dip them into paint to about half the bristle length to avoid paint getting on the ferrule (the little metal piece attaching the bristles to the handle), which can result in fraying. A frayed brush will cause uneven dots, lines, or paint. Keep a cup of water at your work space so you can quickly swish off paint from brushes after use and keep the brushes moist until you wash them thoroughly with soap and water.

Clear Finish

A protective finishing varnish can save time and preserve your art. Available at craft or hardware stores, it is quick and easy to use, and adheres to all parts of the stone evenly. Choose the matte style to help prevent light reflection created by some paints or markers. I prefer to use the spray-on type instead of a brush-on, so I do not need to touch (and potentially smudge) the stone, in case it isn't completely dry.

Finishing spray has many uses. Complete your artwork sooner by spraying it and allowing it to dry at key points in the process so that you can handle your stone between applying coats of gel pen and paint. To prevent pencil mixing with white primer paint, spray clear finish over the pencil and allow it to dry before painting. A final coating when your art is complete will protect against fading, and make it resistant against water and weather.

Spray your finish in a well-ventilated room or outside. Allow your stone to sit at least a day for the finish and the art to dry entirely.

Some paint pens, permanent-ink pens, and gel pens can blur or smear when finishes are applied. Be sure to test this before using them on your stone. Use your pens to color and draw lines over a coat of paint on a stone. Test the spray when ink is still damp as well as when it is completely dry on both light and dark backgrounds. If the ink reacts with the finish, it will blur into the colors around it. If this happens, use a different type of finish or consider other pens or paints.

Fixing Mistakes and Other Tips and Tricks

Oops! We all make mistakes, but think positive! Mistakes can be fixed or avoided with a little planning.

Erasing Mistakes

Many acrylic paint and gel pen colors are opaque enough to paint over other colors and backgrounds without the original colors showing through. This is what makes the base color your friend! Use it as an "eraser" for small mistakes. For wet paint or ink mistakes, wipe them away with water and a brush or cotton swab. If paint is dry, try lightly scraping the mistake off with fine sandpaper or an old emery board, then clear away any dust before painting the area with the underlying base coat color.

Blocking

Use masking tape to block off areas that you don't want to paint. Create crisp, clean paint lines using tape and a utility knife. Layer five or six strips of tape on top of each other on a cutting board. Use a utility knife to slice the tape into thin strips that you can peel off for individual use. Firmly press the strips where you want the lines to be on the stone, then paint over them. Allow it to dry, then peel off the tape.

Patience

Painted stones can take many hours, if not days, to complete. Patience is key. If you rush, you may make mistakes that could have been avoided. That being said, don't worry too much about tiny imperfections. Often in the grand scheme of things they go unnoticed with all the other details around them, and they make your rocks unique.

Painting Dots

Hold the dotting tool in one hand as you would a pencil, and, if needed, steady the rock with your other hand. Try to hold the stick vertically to the stone, coming in at a 90-degree angle when applying dots. Steady your aim by resting your hand, wrist, or elbow against the desk or the stone itself.

To increase the size of each dot from one row to the next is mostly a matter of having the right amount of paint on the sized stick. Usually the smaller the point, the smaller the dot will be. I use the small pointed end of a toothpick. Other ways to achieve very small dots would be to use the very tip of the longest bristle in a round paintbrush. You can always sharpen one end of your dotting tool to make it a smaller point.

When you want to go up in the size of a dot, you can use the same size dotting tool saturated in slightly more paint and add just a bit more pressure while touching the stick to stone. If you do not wipe the paint from the stick before redipping, it will start to dry and accumulate, enlarging the end of the tool. A bigger tool end will also give a bigger dot.

A Steady Hand

You need a relatively steady hand to apply paint or ink precisely, and there are things you can do to help you stay smooth and stable. Keep the area of the stone you are working on directly in front of you and turn the stone as you go. Don't lift the stone: hold it still with one hand and anchor your other hand by placing your pinkie finger on the desk as you paint and draw.

When drawing, move your arm, not your wrist. Just remember, "Pull curves and push straights." Your wrist naturally curves when it bends inward, so it feels more natural to "pull" down curves toward you and to "push" up away from you for straight lines. Paints and inks have varying degrees of thickness and consistency, and the surface of your stone also factors into how you use your tools. You may also need to compensate for tiny holes or other imperfections.

Try to be focused, relaxed, and, if possible, uninterrupted when you work. Control your breathing: don't hold it. Take a deep breath before moments that require the utmost precision.

Hand-lettering

Creating nice lettering attracts attention, no matter what the words say. Use it as an opportunity to send a message worth reading.

The messages in the rock-painting activities in this book are created by hand-lettering. Hand-lettering is the art of drawing letters, as opposed to writing them. It shares many of the same principles as calligraphy (handwritten, follows established rules and alphabets, uses nib and ink) or brush lettering (letters made with a brush or brush-pen), and is often mistakenly called "typography." While typography involves turning an alphabet into a uniform typeface that is usually digitized and can be used repeatedly, hand-lettering is typically made for a specific intent and a single use. Despite them being separate disciplines, you can still learn a lot from calligraphy and typography to apply to your hand-lettering. Spacing is one such shared rule. For hand-lettering, the terminology is pretty straightforward. For example, the space separating two horizontal lines of hand-lettered text is called "line spacing." The space between letters can be described using adjectives like "tightness" or "width."

When creating different styles of lettering, keep in mind that different styles can create considerably different moods. Thick, heavy, bold lines can create a dramatic feel, while thinner lines with flourishes make a more fancy and elegant feeling.

The bottom of a letter rests on what's called its "baseline." The parts of the letter that go above this line are called its "ascender," and the parts that go below the line are called its "descender." By shifting a letter's placement above or below the baseline, you can create a playful, informal look. Slanting letters can give a feeling of movement, while adding more space between individual letters creates a light, airy feel.

Commonly used styles of hand-lettering follow the rule "heavy down, light up." Heavy means a thicker, bold line for the downward strokes of letter lines; light means thin, skinny lines as you draw letter lines upward. Also, any crossbar lines should also be light. To practice drawing this, take note of the natural direction your pen must go when you write the letters of a word in cursive form. Go back over the letters with a pencil, then add lines to thicken all the downward strokes. It's as simple as that!

The possibilities for how to hand-letter your message are only limited by its legibility (is it easy to read?) and space restrictions (your stone is only so big), but not your creative imagination (which is unlimited!).

If you're unsure of the basic strokes or the up-and-down motions of cursive writing, a quick internet search will offer plenty of articles with photos, video tutorials, and worksheets. There are tons of tutorials online that teach many types of lettering, with free fonts for inspiration (which you could also always use as stencils), printable practice sheets, and many more tips and tricks to help you become better at your art.

Pencil and Paper

Do all your thinking and designing with pencil and paper first. The activities in this book began on paper, which is a necessary part of the process to ensure that your design will fit on the rock space you have. Work out any potential issues and practice the design.

Once you have sketched the ideas that you want to develop, trace the outline of the rock you are using as your canvas to determine how big or small your design must be. The design must fit, be centered, and not be crowded.

Use your ruler to lightly pencil in baselines (the imaginary line the letters sit on), horizontal guidelines (the space above and below letters/ words), and vertical guidelines (for spacing between letters/words).

Lightly pencil in the basic letter outlines. Make sure to space the letters enough so that they can be thickened and remain balanced as you develop them. You will be using gel pens and permanent markers on the stone, and these tools have bolder lines than your pencil drawing. Also leave enough room for any decorative elements or illustrations that you want to include later.

When the letters are in place, go over them again. Build and sculpt their lines thickly or thinly where needed, and lightly add any flourishes or embellishments, until you have the final sketch outline of the letters or word.

Finally, sketch the basic outline of any other design or illustrations within the remaining space. You don't need to be too detailed, as the details will come when putting the sketch on your rock. You can go over the outline in ink and use an eraser to clean up unwanted pencil lines. Your hand-lettered design should be complete, so that all you need to do is copy it to stone.

Working on Stone

Work from the bottom up, painting base coats, colors, and background images first. Finish with the main design on top. When using bright paints and inks on stone, it helps to first paint a coat of white as a primer to help those bright colors appear as intended. You can use white primer at any point in the design to reduce the need for multiple layers of paint and gel pen.

Let's Go!

Now that we know the basics, let's begin making our own positive designs and rock art! Complete the designs with mindful intent and believe in their message to get the most out of the experience. Use them daily to remind yourself of their encouraging affirmations, and spread their happiness and positivity by giving them to a friend or loved one. Brighten the day of a stranger by leaving them out in the world to be found. Above all else, remain positive and have fun!

Finding Joy

The word "joy" might be short in stature, but it's big in meaning. Joy is the experience of great happiness and pleasure! Everyone is on their own search for happiness; by hiding this rock, you can help someone "find joy" in their day.

YOU WILL NEED:

- Round stone (approx. 3 inches/7 cm wide)
- Pencil
- Eraser
- Ruler
- Compass
- Fine paintbrush
- Medium paintbrush
- Marker: black (preferably chisel-tipped)
- Paint: white, yellow, black, red
- Protective finish

1 Use a ruler to determine the center point of your stone, and mark this point gently with a pencil. Then use a compass to draw a circle that covers the top of the stone as close to the edge as possible. Fill in this circle with an even coat of white paint as primer; once this is dry, paint over the white with yellow as your base color. Allow this layer to dry, then add a second coat of yellow for the best coverage. When the stone is dry enough to handle, paint a bright red border around the yellow circle to cover the visible sides of the stone when you look at it from above. You'll add a second coat during the final touch-up.

HANDY HINT

If this is your first time lettering, it's easier to practice perfecting your design first on paper before you try it directly on the rock. This will help you get used to the feel and effect of different pens and markers, and perfect smooth-flowing lettering before finalizing the design on your rock.

2 Lightly sketch the outline of each letter on the stone. The lettering in this design is done in a block-letter style, with thick vertical lines and thin horizontal lines—the parts of letters that curve, like the flick of the "j" and the "y" descender, look much more angular, and so does the dot of the "j."

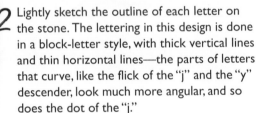

HANDY HINT

To help you keep your lettering straight and even, with the letters' tops and bottoms all at the same height, you can lightly draw horizontal and vertical guidelines onto your yellow circle using a ruler and pencil before you start sketching.

3 When you're happy with your sketch, fill it in using your black marker. Once it's dry, lightly pencil the bordering design around the edge of the stone—a quirky, filigree-style shape with dots and hearts for decoration. I've placed the hearts so that their pointed ends sit in the dips and curves of the filigree pattern, but this design is filled with whimsical personality, so do what feels right to you! Next, use your black marker or black paint to fill in the decorative border shapes. The simple black motif really makes your design pop against its yellow background, meaning its joy is likely to be clear from afar! Try to keep the shapes within the yellow circle.

4 Once the black has dried, use the same bright red paint as before to color the hearts in the design, and use a dotting tool to add lines of small dots to the filigree border. Tapering your dots from bigger to smaller gives them a fanciful look. Also paint a second coat of red over the stripe around the design, to clean up any shapes that may have gone outside the yellow circle. Use yellow paint to clean up and straighten lines over the rest of the stone design. Allow all the paint to dry. Use your black marker to draw smaller black hearts inside the red ones, and finally, add red dots to the tip of your filigree curls. Once the stone is dry again, spray it with one or two coats of protective finish, and admire your lovely artwork!

HANDY HINT

Make sure you've tested for any reaction between the protective finish and your markers or paint before you begin!

Pocket Rock

Gratitude is said to be the precursor to happiness—not just saying "thank you" to others, but truly appreciating what you have. This little "pocket rock" can be carried with you everywhere as a reminder to always stay positive and be thankful for the good things in your life, even in tough times!

YOU WILL NEED:

- Stone
  (approx. 2 inches/5 cm wide)
- Pencil
- Eraser
- Ruler
- Fine paintbrush
- Marker: black
- Paint: white (optional), black
- Gel pens: purple, pink, gold, green, orange
- Protective finish

1 Pencil a guideline across the center to use as the baseline, then draw the letters for "Grateful" in a bold, brush-pen style of hand-lettering, making the downward strokes thicker than the upward strokes. Trace over the penciled letters using black marker or paint, then erase any remaining pencil marks.

HANDY HINT

This design doesn't use a base color because the stone I used was already a very light shade. If you've chosen a darker stone, you can use white paint to prime the flower petals, if you like, to make their colors extra bright. Or try blending a small amount of white paint into ink from a gel pen before it dries to get a pretty pastel shade.

2 Sketch large, ruffled-petal flowers and leaves to fill up the space around the word. The largest flower should cover the entire space below the word. Use the marker or paint to trace over your floral design with a thin black outline.

3 Now add the color! Start by using a pink gel pen to partially fill inside the petals. Use a purple gel pen to edge along the tips of each pink petal, then blend the purple into the pink using a dry paintbrush.

4 Add gold dotted gel-pen highlights around the center of the flowers and inside each of the flowers' pistils. Color the leaves in different shades of green, with darker green veins and outlines. Add some thin, gold gel-pen lines throughout to highlight the colors, and color the area around the lettering gold as well so that the entire word is encased.

5 When your color is dry, carefully trace the outlines in black using a fine paintbrush (or a black fine-tipped marker), do any necessary touch-ups of color, and add in any little lines of detail or decoration you choose. Once the stone is dry again, spray it with one or two coats of protective finish, and admire your lovely artwork!

Always Shine Brightly

Be your own sunshine—your best version of yourself—and send your positive energy beams out into the world! Remember: a candle can light another candle without losing its own light. Cast your own light into the world with this brightly painted mandala stone.

YOU WILL NEED:

- Round stone (approx. 2.5 inches/6 cm wide)
- Pencil
- Ruler
- Eraser
- Compass
- Fine paintbrush
- Marker: black (perferably round-tipped)
- (optional) Dotting tools: small, medium, large
- Paint: black, yellow
- Gel pens: gold, orange, pink
- Protective finish

1 A round stone is a good fit for both the mandala-style art in this design, and to represent the sun! Use a ruler to determine the center point of the stone, and from this point, use a drawing compass to help you draw a large circle that covers almost to the edge of the stone's outline. Then adjust the compass to draw another, smaller circle within this larger circle. This circle should be large enough to contain the words "Shine bright," while still leaving room for the mandala shapes in the outer circle. Paint the inner circle yellow and the outer circle black for the base coat. Allow to dry.

2 Use a ruler and pencil to divide your rock into 16 equal parts by drawing lines through the center of the stone. (It doesn't have to be 16, as long as it's an even number.) These guidelines will help you create your mandala shape.

HANDY HINT

You can adjust some letters in "Shine" so that they drop a bit below the baseline, but without interfering with the word below—I have done this where the "h" connects to the "i." Use an eraser to make any adjustments to the letters so that they are proportionate and spaced evenly.

3 Sketch the word "Shine" in brush-style lettering to fill the top of the yellow circle. Keep the letters thick with smooth curves; try to make the word look smooth, like one continuous brushstroke. Dot the "i" with a star for added cuteness. In the bottom portion of the circle, sketch the word "BRIGHT" in a tall, thin lettering style using all capital letters. Taper the word to fit into the half-circle space (make "B" and "T" the same shorter size, while "I" and "G" should be the tallest letters in the center). Round the bottom of each letter so that it fits in line with the circle's edge. Use a fine paintbrush to fill your lettering in black paint, or use your marker.

4 Fill the center of the letters with gold gel pen, leaving some black visible to border the edges. Allow the ink to dry.

5 Use a compass and pencil to lightly draw three or four more circles on the black base coat, getting incrementally larger as they reach toward the edge of the stone. Begin sketching the mandala at the edge of the center circle. Start with a wavy line that connects to the circle. Turn the stone around as you sketch the mandala row by row. Then add some evenly spaced drop shapes above the wavy line. Continue each new line with a new shaped pattern, such as arcs and pyramids, as depicted. You should have the same amount of shapes in each section, and they should all be the same height and width. Add a final inverted drop shape with accompanying dot for the last layer of pattern to represent the sun's rays. Use white paint to create white scalloping around the yellow circle.

6 From the central arc pattern, paint the teardrop shape pattern. The teardrop shapes should start at the point where the two arcs in the inner pattern meet, and stop around 0.4 inch (1 cm) before the edge of the black circle. Then carefully paint a white outline for each of these teardrops starting at the outer edge of one arc and finishing on the outer edge of the following arc in the sequence.

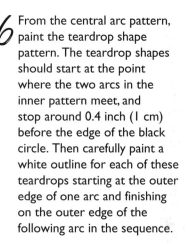

7 Using more white paint, paint the wide, short pyramid shapes between the outlined teardrops facing the opposite way (so the points of the pyramids face toward the center). Make sure that you leave a boundary of black around each drop so that it does not bleed into the side outlines of the teardrops, and doesn't quite meet the top boundary of the teardrops. Still using white, add the little diamond shapes to the tip of the longer teardrop shapes. Then add a dot directly below the point of each diamond shape. From the bottom of each pyramid shape, leave a slight gap, and then paint the other pyramid outline that faces the opposite direction (out toward the rim of the stone).

8 Add a little black triangle outline within these triangles, and finally add a smaller white pyramid. When all paint is dry, it's time to begin coloring your mandala! The first mandala ring of little bumps should be gold. Then the long teardrop shapes should be yellow, with their outlines and diamond tips gold.

9 Paint the pyramids pink, the outer triangle yellow, and the inner triangle orange. When the paint dries and you have added any extra layers of pen and paint as needed, you can add further details in paint or gel pen: add a line of orange dots to the teardrops, alternate darker pink lines to the first layer of the pyramids, add orange dots to the outer-rim dots, and lastly outline with black paint or permanent marker. Allow to dry, and cover your gorgeous, sunny stone with one or two coats or protective finish to keep it shining forever.

Keep on Believing

Keep on believing in yourself with a little encouragement from this beautiful unicorn art piece! Simple determination can overcome incredible odds, while self-confidence and how we talk to and treat ourselves is often the difference between success and failure. If that's not magic, I don't know what is!

YOU WILL NEED:

- Stone: ideally flat and circular (approx. 3 inches/8 cm wide)
- Pencil
- Eraser
- Compass
- Marker: black (optional)
- Fine paintbrush
- Medium paintbrush
- Paint: black, white, gold, and pastel colors of your choice
- Fine glitter and stick-on gem (optional)
- Protective finish

1 Use your compass to draw a circle in pencil as an inside border for your stone. Fill in the circle with a white base coat. Allow to dry. Inside the circle, use the compass to draw four more circles to make your rainbow border, with each circle about 0.1 inch (3 mm) from the last line, and getting smaller as you go inward. Sketch in the outline of the unicorn, with its mane and horn running over the rainbow border but staying inside the outer circle. Erase the inner three circle lines at the bottom left of the stone and sketch the words "Believe in yourself" in the erased area. Use black paint or marker to outline your design lines, details, and lettering, and allow this to dry.

2 Now begin to color! Fill in the sunny yellow background first, then each strand of the rainbow—which can go progressively over the back of the stone, down toward the bottom. Be careful while you handle the stone, as there are a lot of colors near the edge! Make sure each new layer is dry before you continue.

3 Use lots of pretty pastel colors for the unicorn's mane. Make sure there is not too much of the same color all together in the intertwined strands of its glorious mane. You can add highlights of different colored markers to each strand.

HANDY HINT

If you like, you can add a little sparkle to your unicorn by sprinkling a pinch of fine, shimmery glitter (available from your local craft or dollar store) onto the last coat of finish before it dries. Don't add the glitter before the protective finish, though—you'll dull the sparkle! Once the finish dries, you can also add small stick-on gems, if you wish, for an even more magical effect.

4 Add a smudge of blush on the unicorn's cheek. This can be made by fingerprinting your finger with a pink gel pen and then pressing it gently on the white of the unicorn's face. Fill in the holes within your letters and connections between letters with pink outlines, and fill in the rest of the remaining lettering banner in yellow highlighter. Finally, add the crowning glory of the unicorn's golden horn of positivity, and some cheerful pink dots in the background. Once the paint has dried, go back over the design and correct any crooked lines, add second coats of color as needed, and refresh the black outlines with marker or paint. Allow your touch-ups to dry, then finish your artwork with one or two coats of protective finish.

Keep Rockin'!

Hey, you rock! Yes, you! Kind words don't cost anything but can be worth a lot—giving sincere compliments helps strengthen relationships, build trust, and create happy vibes for both the giver and receiver. This rock pays a solid compliment that is sure to put a smile on anyone's face!

YOU WILL NEED:

- Stone, ideally circular (approx. 3 inches/8 cm in diameter)
- Pencil
- Eraser
- Compass
- Fine paintbrush
- Medium paintbrush
- Small dotting tool
- Paint: black, red, orange, yellow, green, blue, purple, lilac
- Protective finish

1 Using a medium paintbrush, paint the front surface of your rock with a dark base coat color—black, navy, or a deep purple would work well. Make sure you paint right to the edge.

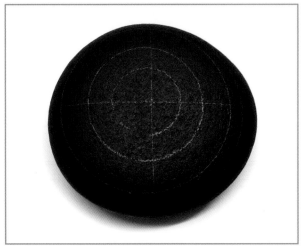

2 When the base coat has dried, use a pencil to create circular guidelines for your lettering and dotting. Use a compass to create four concentric circles that become larger as you go out. The distance between each of the three circles is about double the one before, and the distance between the third and fourth circle is much smaller than the others.

3 Use the first three circles to sketch the words "You Rock!" centered on the stone, in a jaunty lettering style. Make sure the words take up most of the front of the stone. Erase and redraw until you are happy with it.

4 Use a fine paintbrush to fill in your lettering with yellow paint. Once this dries, add a second coat of yellow to the hand-lettering to really make it pop, and then allow it to dry again.

5 Use a small dotting tool to fill up the background with lots of small dots in different colored rings. The dots can be in different sizes, but try to keep them all under 0.1 inch (3 mm). Begin in the center, work outward around the lettering, and fill the stone to its edge. Use the circle guidelines to help you color the rings. This rainbow begins with dark purple in the center, then a lighter shade of purple (lilac), blue, green, yellow (in that thin ring around your text), orange, and finishes at the edge with bright red. Set the stone aside to dry.

6 Place dots of darker yellow paint inside each letter and the exclamation mark. While this dries, place larger dots (about 0.1 inch [3 mm] wide) of yellow paint around the edge of the stone where the colored dots end. Finally, add tiny dots of gold gel pen to each yellow dot in the letters. Go over your rockin' piece of art to see if there's anywhere that needs a second coat of dot paint or black outline. Allow to dry, spray with one or two coats of protective finish, and it's ready to rock!

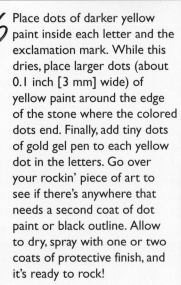

Peace Is an Inside Job

The lotus flower is a symbol of inner peace—rooted in the mud, it grows up through dark, uncertain water to blossom in the light. As this rock says, "Sky above, earth below, peace within." It's a beautiful reminder that in the midst of life's noise, problems, and hard work, we can still have peace in ourselves!

YOU WILL NEED:

- Stone: ideally round or oval (approx. 2.5–3 inches/ 6–8 cm wide)
- Pencil
- Eraser
- Ruler
- Compass
- Fine paintbrush
- Permanent marker: black, white (optional)
- Paint: black, white, light yellow, orange, pink, blue
- Gel pens: purple, pink, blue
- Protective finish

HANDY HINT

Keep your pencil lines light and have your eraser handy until you have the design looking symmetrical.

1 Use a compass to draw a large circle in pencil almost to the edge of your stone. About 0.4 inch (1 cm) inside this, draw another circle. Inside the smaller circle, lightly pencil in a large peace sign—like the shape of the symbol to the left below—using a ruler. This will help you with the placement of the lotus flower and words. Begin drawing the lotus petals along the center line: the tips of all petals go into the circle border slightly; it is only the top petal that reaches the outer circle. The petals above it should be the same size, but pointing upward and stopping short before reaching the sma[ll] circle. Above this, add another, slightly wider petal with its point touching the edge of the circle. Lightly draw four more petals on each side. The larger petals at the bottom begin along the peace sign lines, with the tips pointed out to the left and right respectively. The petals above should be drawn slightly layered with their tips pointed upward; these are the petals that will contain the words. Place in your rough letterin[g] using a slightly wavy but easy-to-read style. The words at the top and bottom of the design look best in all capitals, while the text at the center looks better as mixed capitals and lowercase letters. Paint the design and border with white bas[e] coat and trace over the lines with black permanent marker.

2 Using gel pens, color the border green at the top, blending into blue at the bottom (you can use a paint base underneath and gel pens over the top, smudging them together). Use the black marker or paint to trace the words "Peace within" across the stone, containing each word in the two petals nearest to the center. Work the inner lines of the petals into the lines of the first and last letters of each of the words, so that the last "e" in "peace" joins seamlessly with the petal line on the left side, and the "w" of "within" does the same on the inside right. You can also do this with the letters nearest the circle on both sides.

3 In between the two circles around the edge of the stone, draw the words "SKY ABOVE" at the top of the circle and "EARTH BELOW" at the bottom, all in capitals. Center the words. Once your lettering is penciled in where you want it, trace over it using white paint or permanent marker. Trace around the edges of the petals, one at a time, with purple gel pen. Before this outline dries, use a brush to smudge the ink along the insides of the petals. Highlight the petals that contain the words in light yellow blended into orange and pink segments. Color the remaining petals with pink and purple gel pens, smudged with white to make them pastel-colored, and with a little yellow at their center.

4. Allow to dry, then add a second coat of color or highlighting if needed. Add lines of light yellow dots along the parts of the peace line that lie within the lotus petals. On the inside of the petal outlines, put dots of the same color as that section of the petal (so orange for the top part of the "Peace" petal, etc.). Refresh the black outlines of the lotus petals and the lettering, if required, with black marker or paint. Ensure that your lines and color shading are even, add any other color blends or other details to the lotus that you want to include, and allow to dry.

5. When all is dry, turn the stone on its side and add a final border of two rings of dots. Make the one closest to the lotus yellow, and the one farthest away orange. You can also add some final blue dots to the center of the petals that don't contain the peace sign or the lettering. Don't forget to apply one or two coats of protective finish to protect your gorgeous lotus artwork, so that it will be able to spread its peaceful message for a long time to come!

Dream Rock

Never underestimate the power of dreams to motivate you—dream, and dream big! As you create this intricate rock, think about who you are and who you want to be. What are you truly passionate about? With this dreamy rock, you can inspire others to be "boulder" too!

YOU WILL NEED:

- Stone: ideally circular (approx. 3.5 inches/9 cm in diameter)
- Pencil
- Ruler
- Eraser
- Compass
- Dotting tools: small, medium, large
- Permanent marker: gold (optional)
- Paint: black, white, blue, green, yellow, orange, pink, and purple
- Gel pen: gold
- Protective finish

1 Find the center point of your stone, and from this point, use a compass to draw a large circle to the edge of the stone. Fill the circle with black paint as the base color. Allow the paint to dry, then pencil the outline of the word "Dream" across the center of the stone and outline it with white paint.

2 Use a dowel or other large dotting tool to form a large dot of white paint in the center of the stone, 0.4 inch (1 cm) or larger. Try and make this center dot as close to a perfect circle as possible.

3 Use a small dotting tool dipped in white paint to carefully create a ring of dots all the way around the center circle. Each dot should be no larger than 0.4 inch (1 mm). Space the dots evenly around the circle without touching. The number of dots is important, as it will determine the number of colors you can use for each section: having an even number allows for equal color distribution. The final spiral design here has 30 dots, to make five sections of six different colors.

4 Moving farther out from the center, paint another ring of white dots, slightly larger than the previous row. Stagger the dots' placement so that they're in line with the small spaces left between the dots of the previous ring. Turn the stone as you dot, to get the best view for alignment. Remember, don't rush! Placing dots correctly, as well as gradually increasing their size with each new ring, will help create the harmonious effect of this design.

HANDY HINT

If you find you have trouble evenly spacing your dots, it can help to mark the spots with a pencil first, and once you're happy with all the dots' placement, paint over them.

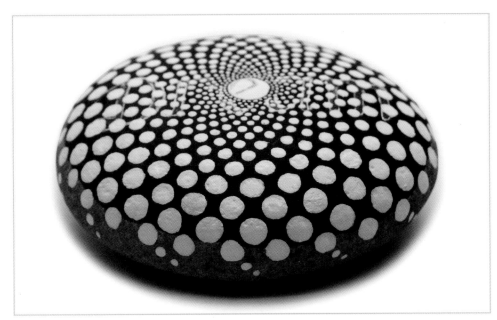

5 Continue adding rings of dots in this manner. As you begin each new ring, increase the size of the dots slightly while maintaining even spacing between each dot and their proximity to the dots in the ring before them. Continue adding rings of dots in this way until you have covered your stone to the edge. Finish off the design by tapering off the dots (making them smaller) in the last few rings of the spiral over the edge.

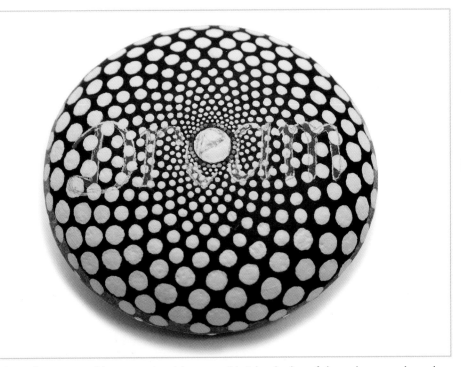

6 Now it's time to add some color. I have used bright shades of the colors purple, red, orange, yellow, green, and blue—in that order. That means painting the first dot using purple, the next with red, then orange, yellow, green, and blue. Begin painting the smallest dots around the center circle. Repeat the color pattern until the ring is complete. Whatever colors you use, make sure you keep them in the same order as you repeat the pattern. A handy way to remember the order is to put the paint itself in that order.

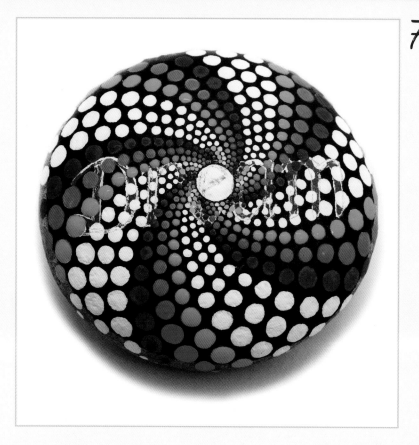

7 When you move on to next ring of dots, shift the color pattern one dot over in a counterclockwise direction from where you began in the ring before. This means placing the blue dot above and to the left of the blue dot in the ring before it. Continu the color pattern until the ring is complete. Then continue shifting the colors one dot over when you begi a new ring. After you have colored three or four rings i the repeating color pattern, you should start to see where each individual color has its own curved path toward the edge of the stone You can now save some time by painting each color (i.e., all blue dots, then green, and so on), rather than alternatin colors dot by dot for each single ring.

8 Once the paint is dry, hold the stone out and away so you can more easily see the swirling visual effect this pattern has and whether there are any dots that are making it a little wonky that you could touch up to be a bit larger, smaller, or better aligned.

HANDY HINT

For this design I have used paint for the different colored dot work, but you can also create the different dot colors by using just white paint and then, once the paint is completely dry, coloring the dots with gel pens.

You should still be able to see some of the white lettering beneath the paint; fill in the letters with white paint and let them dry. Then outline the letters with a gold gel pen. Once everything is dry, apply one or two layers of protective finish. Now your dream has come to life!

HANDY HINT

This stone already looks dreamy, but you can take it up one more level by using a permanent marker to add tiny dots of gold in all the little spaces immediately above each dot. Do this moving from the outer edge to as far in toward the center as you can without touching any other dots.

Stick to It!

Did you know some cacti can survive hundreds of years in harsh deserts, using water stores in their stems and other clever water-saving tricks? Their prickly skin is just their way of protecting themselves. Like a cactus, your inner reserves will see you through, too! So, no matter how bad things get, don't desert your goals—keep going and keep growing!

YOU WILL NEED:

- Oval stone (approx. 2.5 inches/ 6 cm wide)
- Pencil
- Ruler
- Fine paintbrush
- Medium paintbrush
- Paint: yellow, black, white, neon green, dark green
- Gel pens: orange, red, gold, purple, pink, yellow, neon orange
- Protective finish

1. In the bottom part of the stone, pencil in the outline of the cacti's planter box, where the words will go. It should be about 2 x 1.2 inches (5.5 x 3 cm). Once you're happy with the shape, go over the outline in black paint using a fine paintbrush. Then, paint the planter along the edges in a bright terra-cotta color, which you can make by blending orange, red, and gold gel pens, then a little yellow paint that has had a tiny amount of black paint added to it to darken the shade. Fill the middle of the planter box with a lighter, more golden yellow, and blend and fade the darker color in toward the center. Let the paint dry, then sketch in your lettering. Take your time and be patient, as this can be tricky! Draw in pencil "KEEP GOING" across the top of the planter box, using slanted capital letters to give a sense of movement. If you find spacing out the letters awkward, you can use your ruler to mark lines for them about 0.2 inch (5 mm) apart. In the middle section, pencil the words "DON'T STOP." Each letter should be smaller than the last one, to fit into the slanted space. Slant the bottom of each letter along your penciled line, too. Do the same thing in reverse with the word "GROWING" in the bottom section of the rectangle. Start small and increase the height of each letter, and give each one a slanted top.

2 Using a fine paintbrush and black paint or a black permanent marker, trace over the lettering. Once it's dry, you can erase any remaining pencil guidelines and lettering.

3 Now sketch in the outlines of a few different cacti of different heights. When you're happy with your drawing, trace over the outlines in black paint. Then use a purple gel pen to start coloring in the background, starting around the edge of the stone.

4 Fill in the rest of the background first using a pink gel pen, and then an orange gel pen, blending the colors into each other a little.

5 Use a yellow gel pen to highlight the area around your cacti for a glowing effect.

6 Next, use a yellow gel pen to draw sunray lines from your cacti, then add an extra coat of color to the entire background to make it really vivid. Color over the top of the yellow sunrays with an orange gel pen. Finally, fill in your cacti drawing with white paint, and allow to dry. Then trace over the cacti's lines with black paint again.

7 Color the cacti using neon green paint, with darker green lines and a few white highlights for extra texture.

Now add the finishing touches to your artwork. Add texture to the cacti with green and white dots, and color the flowers using pink and orange dots, and allow to dry. Then use black paint to draw in the thorns and other fine details. Dot the lines of your sunrays in yellow and add a row of yellow dots above and below your lettering in the planter box. A neon orange zigzag underneath the word "GROWING" completes your lush artwork! Once the stone is completely dry, apply two or three coats of protective finish, and dry overnight.

Heart of Zen

With this stone, you have the perfect model to keep your heart blooming with positivity. It's perfect to give to someone special or leave to remind others of the power of love.

YOU WILL NEED:

- Heart-shaped stone (approx. 3 x 2.5 inches/ 8 x 6 cm)
- Pencil
- Eraser
- Ruler
- Fine paintbrush
- Paint: neon pink, yellow, orange, blue, purple, green, black, white
- Pens: green, pink, yellow/ gold or orange
- Permanent marker: black
- Protective finish

1 Use a pencil to lightly draw a heart-shaped outline around the edge of the stone. On this line, sketch a floral wreath of different shapes and sizes of overlapping flowers, leaves, and vines. Within the floral border, draw the word "Love" in a thick, cursive lettering across the center of the stone.

HANDY HINT

A heart-shaped stone is perfect for this project, but if you can't find one, any flat stone will work—you can still just use the heart outline as a border.

2 Fill the floral designs and the lettering with white paint as a primer, and allow to dry. You should still be able to see the white outlines. Use black paint or permanent marker to redraw the outlines.

3 Start adding the colors one at a time (so the paint doesn't dry up). Begin by coloring all the green leaves and all other green things in the design, then use pink to color all the pink areas—including the inside of "Love." You can use pink paint or a pink gel pen—pen often works best for smaller spaces where the nib gives you greater control to stay within the outlines. Allow the paint to dry.

4 Continue with the remaining colors, refreshing the black outlines as you go. Choose a selection of bouquet flowers that works best for you. Here I have gone with bright orange, yellow, and pink, with the blue and green providing a useful contrasting tone. Little highlights can really add to your design; for example, use yellow at the center of a flower, then extend the color slightly out into its petals. You can add multiple coats if you want to strengthen the colors.

5 Add second coats of paint and adjust color combinations where you feel
they're needed. A little pink paint rubbed into the area around the lettering
is a pretty finishing touch, and suggests the spread of love. Refresh all the
outlines. Protect your lovely piece with two or three coats of protective
finish, and allow to dry thoroughly. You are ready to give the gift of love!

 # Bee Positive

Bees are industrious little creatures—humming along, focused, and working happily all day. Did you know that when you work with a positive mind-set, your productivity, creativity, and social engagement all improve, even in difficult situations? Take it from the bees: stay positive and remember to stop and smell the flowers!

YOU WILL NEED:

- Stone: (approx. 2.75 inches/ 7 cm in diameter)
- Pencil
- Ruler
- Fine paintbrush
- Medium paintbrush
- Paint: white, black, yellow
- Gel pens: gold, pink, orange, purple, red, blue, green
- Fine-tipped black permanent marker
- Protective finish

1 Choose a wide stone. On the left side or top center of your stone (depending on how much space you have), use a pencil to lightly draw a flying honeybee, followed by the looping word "positive," as if this word is the bee's flight. Draw the letters without worrying about keeping them in line (bees don't fly straight anyway), adding an extra loop here and there. Connect the line to your bee with a looping line to the "p" as a flourish. Make sure that the bee is proportionate to the letters and the spacing is equal across the stone. Underneath, draw flowers in different shapes and sizes. No need to be too detailed: just have an idea what you can use here to fill the area.

2 Apply a base coat of white over all your flowers, bee, and lettering, and then retrace the outlines as necessary. This will help the colors you put on top really pop.

3 Use a gold or yellow gel pen and alternate with a black permanent marker to create your happy honeybee. Yellow is also perfect to make your "positive" bee path stand out, and to highlight sunny flowers. Use your other favorite bright colors for the other flower petals (here I've used purple, blue, and orange), and use a lush green marker for their leaves and stems. When you're finished, you can use a fine-lined black marker to trace the outline of the letters, giving a bit of extra thickness to the downstrokes. You can also outline any of the flowers you wish to be clearer. Finally, spray with two or three coats of protective finish and leave to dry.

4 If you want to, you can make this stone double-sided! Once the first side is completely dry, add extra protection by covering it with plastic wrap while you work on the other side. Use a pencil to continue the last line of the "e" from "positive" around to the other side of the stone. It should run loopily from the left side into the center, to then meet "be" on the other side of the rock. You can make the "be" with a dashed line, emphasizing the bee's flight. Then write "Kind" in fancy lettering that loops like a vine. The "K" has a long curlicue that extends down under almost the whole word, and another flourish twirls from the "d" inward, over the top.

5 Draw a small daisy to dot the "i," and add some more little flowers along the swirls coming off the letters. Go over the lettering, bee, and flower flourishes in a white primer. Once dry, add color using gel pens, using the same gold or yellow color for the bee, green for "Kind," and your choice of color for the flowers. It works well to leave the bee's path, little eye circle, and wings white; the petals of the flowers can be left white as well, if you would like them to be daisies. When all is dry, you can apply black marker outlines, like you did to the first side. Apply two or three coats of finishing spray and allow to dry.

A Little Becomes a Lot

Every little choice we make—every single thing we do—matters. So don't undervalue tiny decisions and small acts of kindness! You never know what effect they'll have. What you can be sure of is that your little kindnesses, even something as small as words on a rock, will grow and multiply out in the world. It's like magic: little by little, they become a lot!

YOU WILL NEED:

- Round stone (approx. 3 inches/8 cm wide)
- Pencil
- Eraser
- Ruler
- Fine paintbrush
- Medium paintbrush
- Permanent marker (optional): black
- Paint: black, white, gold, green, orange, pink, purple
- Protective finish

1 Use a pencil to draw a circular outline at the rim of your stone, and another circle just in from the first. Then use a ruler to lightly pencil in the arrows, intersecting in an "X" shape to the edges of your outline. Next, lightly pencil in parallel, crossing lines to make the diamond shapes inside the "V"s created by the arrows. To ensure that the lines are evenly spaced and each side exactly mirrors the other, you can draw the lines to fill the entire circle and erase the ones that you don't need. Draw two pairs of horizontal lines across the center of your stone with a ruler, to create top and bottom borders for your lettering, then pencil the words "little BY little" inside these. Place the "BY" in the very center, with the letters split left and right of the arrows, and put "little" on either side.

2 Fill in the areas you're going to color with white paint as primer, and trace over the letters with white paint as well. Select individual diamond shapes in the top "V." Allow to dry. Then, using a fine paintbrush and black paint, trace over the lines and diamond shapes you want to keep. In the bottom, trace only the first four lines in both directions.

3 Use a fine paintbrush to fill the shapes with color, as shown. Paint one color at a time, and use a gold gel pen for the borders.

4 Use a dotting tool to add little yellow dots around the outer border and on the arrows, and highlight the lettering with a gold gel pen. Trace over the black outlines again and add second coats of color where needed. When you're happy that all the lines and shapes are straight and even, and all paint is dry, apply two or three coats of protective finish.

Positive Pineapple

A symbol of welcome and hospitality, the pineapple may have a rough, spiky exterior, but it's the sweet interior that really matters! This stone, with its lovable message, is not only an inspiring hide-and-seek rock, but also makes a thoughtful hostess gift nestled in a basket of snacks.

YOU WILL NEED:

- Stone (approx. 5 x 3 inches/ 13 x 8 cm)
- Ruler
- Pencil
- Fine paintbrush
- Medium paintbrush
- Paint: white, black, gold, yellow, green, red
- Permanent marker: black
- Gel pens: gold, red, green, neon green
- Protective finish

1 Choose a large, long stone. Paint it black. Pencil the outline of a pineapple on it and fill the outline with white paint as a primer. When the primer has dried, pencil in the design guidelines: draw lines to separate the pineapple's main body and its leafy crown, and outline the leaf shapes. Use a ruler to lightly pencil vertical center lines from the tip of the top leaf straight through to the bottom of the pineapple, then use this line to help you draw intersecting diagonal lines across the body, creating a diamond pattern.

2 Leaving one or two rows at the top and bottom of the pineapple body, lightly draw guidelines for each line of the text "Be a pineapple: stand tall, wear your crown, & be sweet" in the center of the pineapple. Sketch in the basic letter shapes. You can see that the hand-lettering I've used is different for each line of text, and the words with more emphasis are shaped differently. The word "pineapple" is large and bold at the top and arcs as if it's being pushed up by the word "tall" below it—which is drawn in a tall, thin lettering. For the "w" in "crown," draw a simple crown shape; the word "sweet" is cursive and cute, with a bit of flourish. The smaller words are stacked to free up space. Don't forget to include the punctuation!

3 Paint the entire pineapple body yellow for the main background base color. Paint right over the top of the pencil sketch. You will still be able to see the sketch through a single coat of yellow paint. Fill the leaves with a green background base.

4 When the base colors have dried, add more layers until you get the color you want, tracing over the pencil of the lettering and lines each time beforehand so you don't lose them. Use black permanent marker to trace over the lettering and leaf outlines. Lightly add some red to the diamond lines of the pineapple.

HANDY HINT

Spray the pencil sketch with a light coat of finish spray so that it does not run into the yellow paint. Use tape to protect the rest of the stone from unwanted paint.

5 In the remaining rows of diamond pattern, loosely sketch horizontal lines that divide the diamonds in half to make two triangles. Make the top triangles look like upside-down heart shapes, and draw vertical lines through the center of the bottom triangles. Add shading to all the lines, especially around the heart curves. Fill in every second little triangle with gold gel pen hearts. Draw the leaves of the pineapple crown in fully using green and gold gel pens for leaf details.

6 For extra zing, add little neon green dots to each intersection of the pineapple diamonds and around its outside border. Then add more green paint dots along the pineapple's leaves, and fill in the "w" of "crown" with yellow. Give your art the final touches as needed: refresh the black outlines, even out any wobbly letterir lines, blend gel-pen color, and so on. When everything is complete and dry, protect your fabulous pineapple art with two or three coats of protective finish.

Congratulations!

Wow! You've positively rocked this. I can already feel the good vibes you've created!

What will you do with your stone art now? Of course, you can keep the stones for your own inspiration. Place them in areas of your home or office where they can be easily seen, to serve as little reminders of what's important in life and what you should focus on when things get tough.

Once you feel they've served their purpose, why not give them as gifts? You may know someone in need of a little positivity—or, if you just want to spread kindness into the world, you can set your stone artworks free outside for anyone to find. The universe will see to it that whoever finds each stone will appreciate it. You can be sure that you've made a difference—and no matter how small, it matters!

Above all, have fun! And remember, true happiness (like peace) is an inside job: one that you need to choose to show up to and work hard at every day. You'll find yourself stuck between a rock and a hard place many times during your life, but with enough practice, you can remain grateful and see the positives in every struggle.

Paint that rock, and use it to give hope and inspiration to others!

About the Author

Katie Cameron is a self-taught artist from the city of Halifax, on the east coast of Canada. She began painting stones in the summer of 2015 after being inspired by the smooth, round stones at nearby beaches. This title is the fourth amazing, do-it-yourself painted-rock book she has written! Katie had this to say about finding her first painted rock:

Finding that rock made me smile, and I didn't stop thinking about it. Without even realizing that I'd been affected by this small act of kindness, I was already paying it forward, leaving my little mandala stones around the neighborhood for others to find. I needed to come up with my own place online for people to find out more about my stones… This is how #hfxrocks was born!

It's pretty neat to think that I am where I am in life today partly because of a chain of events set off by a total stranger who just wanted to paint rocks and use them to make the world a little happier.

Thunder Bay Press
An imprint of Printers Row Publishing Group
10350 Barnes Canyon Road, Suite 100, San Diego, CA 92121
www.thunderbaybooks.com • mail@thunderbaybooks.com

Printers Row Publishing Group is a division of Readerlink Distribution Services, LLC. Thunder Bay Press is a registered trademark of Readerlink Distribution Services, LLC.

Correspondence regarding the content of this book should be addressed to Thunder Bay Press, Editorial Department, at the above address. All other correspondence (author inquiries, permissions) should be addressed to Hinkler Books Ptd Ltd. 45–55 Fairchild Street, Heatherton, Victoria, 3202, Australia

Thunder Bay Press
Publisher: Peter Norton
Associate Publisher: Ana Parker
Editor: Dan Mansfield
Product Manager: Kathryn C. Dalby

ISBN: 978-1-64517-436-3

Printed in China

24 23 22 21 20   1   2   3   4   5